NEWTON
PAGE

NEWTON PAGE

## BIOGRAPHICAL INFORMATION

DANIEL DEFOE (1660-1731) is best known today as the author of the novels Robinson Crusoe (1719), Moll Flanders (1722) and Roxana (1724), but the vast majority of his literary output was as a journalist and pamphleteer. No stranger to controversy and dissent, his writing led to him being arrested, placed in a pillory and imprisoned. An early pioneer of economic and financial journalism, he wrote extensively about John Law and the Mississippi Bubble in Paris, as well as the South Sea Bubble in London. His pamphlets The Chimera: Or, The French Way of Paying National Debts Laid Open (1720), and The Case of Mr. Law Truly Stated, In Answer to a Pamphlet Entitul'd A Letter to Mr. Law (1721) were two of the most significant and insightful contemporary critiques of John Law and the Mississippi Scheme. He constantly battled poverty, and died in London, in debt, hiding from his creditors.

JOHN LAW (1671-1729) was a Scottish economist and financier. Sentenced to death for killing a man in a duel, he escaped his condemned cell and fled to Europe where he became an expert in banking and finance. After the publication of his major work *Money and Trade Considered with a Proposal for Supplying the Nation with Money* (1705) he settled in Paris and founded the Banque Générale (later the Banque Royale) and the Compagnie d'Occident (later the Compagnie des Indies, or Mississippi Company). He used the Banque Royale to implement a policy of exponentially increasing the French money supply which, combined with his public relations activities, fueled frenzied speculation in the shares of his Mississippi Company and gave rise to the first stock market bubble. He became one of the richest men in history, and the term 'millionaire' was coined to describe those who had profited from his scheme. He was appointed Controller-General of Finances—effectively making him the Prime Minister of France—but his successes were short-lived. The stock market bubble soon burst, and both the public and Parlement turned against him. Demands were made for him to be sent to the Bastille and executed. Fearing for his life, he fled France. He spent the rest of his life gambling and justifying the tenets of his Mississippi Scheme to anyone who would listen. He died in relative poverty in Venice.

# THE CHIMERA

# OR, THE FRENCH WAY OF PAYING NATIONAL DEBTS LAID OPEN

by

DANIEL DEFOE

NEWTON PAGE

NEWTON PAGE

www.newtonpage.com

The Chimera:
Or, The French Way of Paying National Debts Laid Open

By

Daniel Defoe

First published by Newton Page 2014

1 3 5 7 9 10 8 6 4 2



ISBN 978-1-934619-10-0

Printed in the United States of America
Set in Adobe Garamond Pro

CONTENTS

# NOTE ON THE TEXT

Since *The Chimera: Or, The French Way of Paying National Debts Laid Open* was first published, conventions of spelling, grammar, punctuation, expression, word-truncation, vocabulary and general notation have each undergone considerable modernization. In addition, the relatively crude assembly practices of early eighteenth-century mass-market pamphlet production have been gradually replaced by the radically more exacting standards of modern publishing, which demand both uniformity of typesetting and editorial consistency. As a consequence of those changes, the modern reader is used to a much simpler, cleaner and polished product than those which were available in the 1720s.

However, notwithstanding the usual expectations of the modern reader, and in full appreciation that the original text is not as easy on the modern eye as it would have been on the early eighteenth-century equivalent, the temptation to edit it to conform with modern writing and publishing conventions has been resisted. That approach has been taken because to do anything other than retain the original form of the pamphlet would be to detract from its inelegant and colorful character and, in turn, serve to dilute the coarse strength of the arguments that such a form proffered to the equally inelegant, colorful and coarse patrons of the coffee houses, inns and taverns in which the original pamphlet would have been so freely read and recited.

There are three minor technical exceptions to the above. First, the archaic long 's', which fell out of favor in the late eighteenth-century, has been removed and replaced with the more familiar and modern short 's'. Secondly, except where inserted to demarcate certain text for the purposes of both ease of reading and separation, the superfluous italics, endemic in most books of the early eighteenth-century, have been removed and replaced with a regular text style. Thirdly, a few minor instances of small capitalization have been substituted for regular capitalization.

Daniel Defoe originally wrote the pamphlet for the consideration of the inhabitants of Great Britain. As such, it is tailored to conform with the conventional eighteenth-century stylistic expectations of a British readership. American readers will notice that in maintaining the integrity of the original publications, the original historic British forms of spelling have been retained. More generally, readers will notice both inconsistent and imaginative forms of spelling throughout the pamphlet.

# THE
# CHIMERA:
## OR, THE
# FRENCH WAY
## OF
# Paying National Debts, Laid open.

BEING

An IMPARTIAL ACCOUNT of the Proceedings in *FRANCE*, for Raising a PAPER CREDIT, and Settling the MISSISSIPI STOCK.

---

*LONDON*:
Printed for *T. Warner*, at the *Black-Boy* in *Pater-Noster-Row*, 1720.

( Price One Shilling. )

# THE CHIMERA

(1720)

# THE CHIMERA:
# OR, THE
# FRENCH WAY
# OF
# Paying National Debts,
# Laid open.

BEING

An IMPARTIAL ACCOUNT
of the Proceedings in FRANCE,
for Raising a PAPER CREDIT,
and Settling the MISSISSIPPI
STOCK.

# AN
# Impartial Account, &c.

It was many Years ago since the French Court regretted very much the hight of the Publick Credit in England, they look'd upon it as the Great, and perhaps the only Advantage that England had over them in the War, Namely, That by the Establish'd Reputation of the Publick Funds here, and the Authority of Parliamentary Credit, whatever Sum of Money was Voted in England, tho' the Funds did not produce it in many Years, and tho' the Loans were prodigiously Great, yet the

Publick could command the Money in a few Days, perhaps in a few Hours; Five and twenty Hundred Thousand Pound Sterling, an Immense Sum told out into French Livres, has been Subscrib'd to the Engraftment of the Bank in a few Hours: Lotteries of a Million have been fill'd before the Lottery itself could be pass'd in Parliament, and before it could be Imagin'd possible to Crowd into the Office, the Tickets have been all Subscrib'd, and the Mony all immediately paid in.

This was as much the Terror of our Neighbours, as it was the Honour and Advantage of England; and Foreigners have been heard to say, That there was no getting the better of England by Battle, No, tho' Victory was always on their side. That while we had thus an inexhaustible Storehouse of Money, no superiority in the Field, could be a Match for this superiority of Treasure; for Money being the Basis of the War, in the Modern way of carrying such things on in the World, it had long since been a receiv'd Maxim in the Case of War, That the longest Purse, not the longest Sword, would be sure to Conquer at last: As in two Mens Boxing, not always he that had the strongest Arm, but he that had the longest Breath, would be sure to have the better of his Enemy.

It was in vain that the late King of France, tho' he had an Absolute Command of the Greatest, and at first the Wealthiest Nation in the World, tryed all the Methods, all the Arts that human Wit could

Invent to raise a Fund of Credit in his Kingdom, and could never bring it to pass; the whole Council of France could never dictate to him the Method how it should be done: This Coy Mistress, call'd Credit, could never be woo'd; the more he pursued her, or the farther he follow'd her, the faster she fled from him; and he had the continual Mortification to see his National Credit fall, even by the same Methods which made our National Credit rise; and as our Credit here grew daily, and at last encreased to such a hight, that from paying Twelve and Fourteen per Cent. for Money, and struggling with infinite Difficulties to get it brought in, we came to reducing the Interest from Six per Cent. to Five per Cent. and now to have the publick Command of what

Money they pleas'd at Four per Cent. and have it brought in faster than they could take it, or had any occasion for it.

It is not possible to set down here, the Schemes, Projects, and infinite Art and, secret Practises which the King of France used to command Credit; all which were disappointed and blown up, by the frequent Exigences of the Publick Affair, forcing him to violate the Faith and Honour of his Edicts, Declaring such or such a Fund of Interest to be Sacred and Unalterable, and not to be stop'd upon any account whatever; and the next Year, or perhaps sooner, breaking thro' all those Sacred Edicts, suppressing the Payment, and leaving the Lenders to Starve: Whereas in England one Parliament always Voted the making good the Deficiencies of another; and no misapplication of Money could be made, but every Fund was kept Sacred to its particular special Appropriation: So that no Man whatever having lent his Money to the Government on the Credit of a Parliamentary Fund, has been Defrauded of his Property.

Thus the Arbitrary Government of the King of France, the Property of every Man being intirely at his Dispose, destroy'd the very Reason and Nature of Publick Credit; and the Limited Power of Great-Britains Crown, the Strings of the Purse being in the hands of the Parliament, whose Appropriations, if I may be allow'd to speak so plain, even our Kings themselves durst not break in upon, has been the Reason and

Foundation of such an immense, boundless Credit, that nothing can hurt or destroy unless the Parliament should Invert their way of acting, and take into their hands the same Absolute Power which it is their business to Restrain, and Wound and Injure themselves, that is to say, the People whom they Represent.

But Fate and the Fortune of France has now turn'd the Tables upon us, and we see the same Arbitrary Power that in the late Reign in France plung'd them into an insuperable Debt, and into an irrecoverable state of Deficiency and Discount, I say, the same Arbitrary Power has rais'd an inconceivable Species of meer Air and Shadow, realizing Fancies and Imaginations, Visions and Apparitions, and making the meer speculations of Things, act all the Parts, and perform all the Offices of the Things themselves; and thus in a moment their Debts are all vanish'd, the Substance is answer'd by the Shadow; and the People of France are made the Instruments of putting the Cheat upon themselves, the Name of the thing is made an Equivalent to the Thing itself, transposing the Debts from the King to themselves, and being contented to Discharge the Publick, owe the Money to one another.

As this is the meer Consequence of a boundless Power in the King by which he is made able to put every Scheme, however impracticable in other places, in a Course of Operation there; so that very Limitation of Power, which is in other Cases our Glory and Advantage, is the Reason why, let our Credit be what it will, our Debts remain, and must be wasted or diminished off, by the slow fire of Parliamentary Proceedings, and by no other way.

And thus for once in the World, Tyranny has the whip-hand of Liberty; for nothing can be done in England like this, even the Parliament it self is limited, and there are its redeemable and unredeemable Funds the last of which are a Burthen, nothing but the Number Ninety Nine (Years) can put an end to: But in France they have an unbounded liberty to act as they please.

Let no Man mistake me here, as if I were bewailing the Incumbrances of National Privileges, and suggesting that it was Pity we should be a Nation of Liberty with such a Burthen of Debt; on the other hand, let us be, say I, a free Nation deep in Debt, rather than a Nation of Slaves Owing nothing; and indeed even in this the Condition of France and England stands in a posture much to our Advantage when compared together, namely France, a Kingdom immensely Rich as a Government, wretchedly Poor as a People; England, a Government Embarrass'd in Debt, Exhausted of Funds, and not able (easily) to get out of Debt; But as a People immensely Rich, Rich in the particular and private Wealths of the Subjects; Poor, that is to say, Encumbred in Debt, speaking of the publick state of Things as a Government, and yet with all this, while the publick Credit remains, we can never be said to be Poor:

But of that in another Place, and on another Occasion.

It remains now, that we look into this flagrant Delusion of paying a Nations Debts, as it is Practising upon the Ignorant People in France: Never in my Opinion, was any Number of People so hook'd in to put a sham upon themselves, and then call it paying off the King's Debts, or the publick Debts; for, as above, 'tis no more and no less, than a parcel of Fools Discharging the King of his Debts, and Owing it to one another. And this is another Reason of this piece of Magic in France, for the very Want of Credit in France, has been the Reason of their obtaining the Credit of paying their Debts. This Paradox shall be unriddled immediately thus: Had not the Publick Credit been bad, had not the State Bills, that is to say, the publick Credit run at Sixty to Sixty three per Cent. Discount, the People would never have brought themselves to part with them for the Bonds, or Shares in a New Company; a Brat of State, which has its Life in the King's Breath, and must die whenever that Breath pleases to determine it, that live by the favour of the King, and Consequently always lives at his Mercy; just thus, turn the Tables again, I say, just thus stands the Case in England Reverst, the goodness of the Publick Credit in England, is the reason why we shall never be out of Debt; for where is the Man that having lent his Money to the Publick on the Credit of Parliamentary Security, will upon a whim, Discharge that Fund, and take a precarious Company of Private Men for the Money.

The Funds are our Security, and we are satisfyed fully in the safety of those Funds, because made Sacred by the Authority of Parliament; this is our advantage who are private Men, and have our Estates there; but this is a blow to the very possibility of paying the publick Debts, because no Man is out of Love with his Security, and because no better Security can be proposed by any Man.

From these Premises, I come down to the very Extraordinary Mr. Laws, a Man, who being first acquainted with the solid Immovable state of Credit in England, and seeing the fluctuating manner of things in France, plainly saw also, how easie it was to push those things there, which he could not so much as think of in England, without apprehensions of being pull'd in pieces by the Rabble.

The first thing Mr. Laws did, who wisely concluded, that a foundation of Credit must be laid before any sufficient Project could be founded upon it, I say, the first thing Mr. Laws did, was to Contemplate the Raising a Royal Bank in France, this he Effected by the Concurrence of the King, whose Sanction there, as the Parliament would be here, was absolutely necessary for such a Work.

Now let the Schemes Engrafted since, or then design'd to be Engrafted upon the foot of this beginning be what they will, whether Knavish or Sincere, as

I will not take upon me here to Determine; yet I say, let it be one way or other, 'tis Evident Mr. Laws made a Right Judgment, and that nothing could be projected for the publick Service of any kind, without an Establish'd Credit to Center some where.

As I have said already, it was impossible this should be grafted upon the Government, the Endeavours to bring it to pass before, having been rendred abortive by the frequent Exigencies of that Government, forcing them to break in upon themselves, mortgage Faith and Honour, Royal Edicts, and Royal Promises, the strongest engagements that could at that time be made; by which means the few Men that had any Money, were made Cautious, and were grown too

Wise to put it into hands which they could not depend upon for the Demand of it again, when it should be wanted.

It remain'd then to resolve, that Credit could now, be only raised upon the forming Societies of Private Men, who were Masters of Cash and able to Support the Credit they took; with whom it might be safe to venture the Deposite of Money, and who by an Exact Currency of payments, might in Consequence, and by Degrees, obtain the name or Title of a safe Fund, and become the Center of proper Credit for the whole Kingdom; a thing at that time greatly wanted, for the advantage of Trade in France, as well as for the Purpose design'd by Mr. Laws. This almost by the nature of the thing, would be called a Bank, and would be managed by the first Adventurers in their own right, and independent of the King or of any Branch of the Government; so that except by meer Plunder, even all one as by Rifling the City of Paris, the King could never lay his hand upon any thing which was put into their keeping.

This was a well lay'd design, had there been no more intended than was pretended. For upon the Credit and Capital Stock of the first Subscribers, there was Immediately a Clear prospect of a Currant Running Cash, Establish'd upon just Foundations, and Sufficient to answer all the business of France; I mean such business as was fit for the managment of a Bank.

When this Scheme was

shew'd to the Regent, he was too penetrating not to see immediately, that it was too Beneficial a thing not to be Encouraged, as well for the Credit of the Nation in General, as for the use of the Government in Particular; and therefore received it with open Arms, and assured Mr. Laws of his Favour and Protection: But this was not all, for every day giving new lights into the thing it self, and new prospects arriving every day, the Regent who begun even then to see that there was nothing which might not be hoped for from such a Design, as well for the Service of the Government as the Advantage of Commerce in General, and of Private Persons interested in it in Particular; for really a Face of publick Credit was a new thing in France, and had so long been Desir'd, and so often Endeavoured without Success, that it look'd like a Dream, and that Man that pretended to undertake it, was like an Angel come from Heaven to bring them good Tidings. From this time forward Mr. Laws, as he well deserv'd, was received with great Distinction, and admitted to such Privacies as became necessary by the Importance of his Undertaking; and as they found his first Scheme Fruitful of great Improvement, he was Encouraged to apply his thoughts Effectually to those Improvements, that something might be brought to pass for the publick good, and Especially to restore Credit to France, a thing the whole Kingdom, but especially as a Government, had suffered many Year for the want of.

In prosecution of this Confidence, the Bank was Established, the Patents or Charter, as we would call it here, were Expedited for its Foundation; the King begins the Subscription, the Duke Regent follows, and innumerable others; they are Impower'd to take in a Hundred Millions Original Stock, and to give out Bills for Currant Cash payable at Demand, and to the Bearer, just after the manner in England; and from that time to this they have acted just as ours do here, are managed by a Court of Directors, for the Governing daily, every incident that may happen, and having preserv'd their Credit in payments Inviolably, it is not easie to conceive what Stocks of Money they have brought into their Hands, and to what monstruous degree of Credit they are already arrived.

Their business is just as it is with our Bank here; they receive and Pay vast Sums of Money for the King and their Bills pass in the Royal Treasury at Ready Money; they have built a New Bureau or Office, and it was a prodigy not often seen in Paris, to see about Three hundred Carriages Loaden with Silver and Gold, carried under the Guard of a party of Dragoons, through the Streets to the new House, where they made a large Vault, which they call the Charter-house, for the keeping it safe, and preserving with it their Writings, Pledges, &c.

They lend Money upon Jewels, Plate, and things of real Value, not Perishable by keeping; and upon Mortgage of Lands at three per Cent. Interest; they Discount Bills, and take in Money, Issuing Bills of Credit payable at Demand; and it is inconcievable the mighty Encrease of business they have upon their hands in so little time, and the immense Sums of Money they have by them in Specie.

Mr. Laws having thus successfully finished this great Affair, was at Leasure to enquire what further Projects might be founded upon this of a Royal Bank: He was too knowing not to have in his Head the General Idea of all those things which have happened since, tho' not perhaps of the Success they have met with, which I cannot but believe have Exceeded his own Expectation: But he that knew that nothing could be done without a Fund of

Credit first Established, knew also that such a Fund of Credit being once thoroughly established, nothing could miscarry that was founded upon it; for as half the Projects in the World fail, and become abortive for want of ready Money and Credit, so when once a Project is backed and supported with a flush of Ready Money, they must be weak Mannagers indeed, if they miscarry; for being well backed, the Execution is in a manner secured.

The first thing of Moment he went upon; was the planting a Collony in the West-Indies, or in North-America; not that Mr. Laws did not know that the Planting the Louisiania; or the Country on the River Missisippi, would not produce any great Effects, at least in his time; for the Settling a Collony; however prosperous in its begining is a Work of time, and must take up not many Years only, but ages of Years; and that the utmost he could have before him in such an Undertaking, was to die in the Faith of its success, and to have the Satisfaction of having his Name very much talked of when he was Dead.

But Mr. Laws, like a Man of just Reach and Penetration, knew that two things would be absolutely necessary to his Design, 1. To have the King approve and Embark in his designs, and, 2. To make his Scheme Popular, to have something in View that should look Capital; have a view and prospect of Success, beyond, not only what he could manage, but even beyond what he ever intended in the Proposal.

Having started the Project of Mississippi, he branch'd it out in a Different manner from all Projects; for he did not descend from the Mississippi Scheme as the General, to the subsequent things as the Particulars; but he ascended from the Mississippi Scheme as a Particular, to a West-India Company as the General; and a General it was, fruitful of many Particulars, every one in themselves capable of as great things, and perhaps greater than the Planting the Colonies of Mississippi was in it self.

When the Company was thus formed, his next work was to propose the Foundation on which they were to be Establish'd, and this was a Subscription of Stock; and here he shewed his first Masterly Stroke, and that he had Concerted all the steps and measures of his Management from the beginning: The Publick Credit in France was still low, nor did the Rising Credit of the Royal Bank add any thing to it, but rather diminish'd, it and let the World see that private Credit in France might revive, but publick Credit could not: The State Bills, and Credits, Annuities on the Town-house, Loans, and all the publick Papers which the Government had Drawn the People in to part with their Money to purchase, were at this time exceeding low, namely from 57, to 63 per Cent. loss, and like to be more; it was the easiest thing in the World to Establish a Fund for any New Undertaking that was but tolerably promising, where the Subscribers could be allow'd to subscribe these Dying

Credits at a Par, and put that into Stock at 100 Livres, which Cost the Purchaser but 37 to 40 Livres per Cent. And this thing alone fill'd his Subscription, which at first consisted of 100 Millions, and was very quickly full.

The first Bite Mr. Laws may be said to put upon the Country was, to give out by way of *premio*, Ten Thousand Pistoles, or thereabouts, at the Rate of — per Cent. for the Refusing of the Mississippi, or West-India Stock, now subscrib'd and full, at 100 Livres each Action for a Years time: This was what we call, The buying of the Bear-skin; and was a dear Bear-skin to those that sold it, as we shall hear presently.

This was the time they begun to banter Mr. Laws: Some said he was Mad, and knew not what to do with his Money; others Laugh'd at him, and said, He was not in England, where he could hedge one way to day, and another way to morrow; could give in the morning and take in the afternoon; And thus they took the Money greedily, not Considering what might be hid under the management of a Man whose Talent they had not yet tryed.

I purposely pass over here the many Movements which Mr. Laws made in this part, to secure to himself the Advance he should get by the Rise of his Stock; for he who had the Power of adding Credit to his Project whenever he pleas'd, had nothing to do but to make sure of the Profits of the first Rise to himself; and therefore he took Care to give out his whole

Sum, as I have heard, of 10000 Pistoles, before he set his other Wheels at work. And after this let us see how he went on:

He had now a Bank of Currant Cash Establish'd on one hand; this he has kept free and unconcern'd in all Adventures or Projects, as what might one way or other shake their Credit; but he kept them perfectly unincumbred, always able to answer all Demands upon them, and to resist every shock that might be made upon them, by the force of their ready Money in specie; none of which he would suffer to be Diminished, except by Loans on sufficient Securities. And I shall give presently an Account how this method was their real Security, and how they had been overthrown at once, by the Chicannry of their and his

Enemies if this Course had not been taken; of which by and by.

He had on the other hand a Subscription of Adventurers, as they might truly be call'd; and as the nature of the thing indeed Imported, whose Stock did not cost them much, being bought as above, with what Cost them not above, 37 to 40 per Cent. and even was not indeed very Currant at that Price neither: These therefore were fit to run any reasonable risque, to embark in any probable Undertaking; to advance the Credit of that Undertaking; and, if possible, to raise their Imaginary Stock, for it was no more at first, to a Real Stock of 100 Livres in Value, for 100 Livres Subscription; and the way how to do this, therefore was the next proper business of the

Company to Consider.

The first thing to be Enquir'd was, to find out something to do, something to Trade in, for as to Planting in Mississippi, tho' that was to be kept going on, as the Denominating Business of the whole; yet it was plain, that Mr. Laws never Design'd a Hundred Millions of Livres should be Employ'd in Peopleing a Wilderness: He therefore turns back to the King, from whom he Received the Life of the whole, and by whose Authority and Business all the Wheels were to be set to Work.

The Publick was a large Field, were one Man has no Credit, and another great Credit; 'tis easy to see who of the two should be the gainer by the other: He that has no Credit can do nothing without

Money, he that has Credit wants no Money tho' he has none.

A Government sunk into Debt, and her Securities bought at 60 per Cent. Discount, gives Room for vast Advantages, where the Party has Money to work with; in a Word the Business was to buy Low, and then bring up the Price of what was bought; namely to buy at 60 per Cent. cost, and then sell at a Par, as we now see is since done.

The King, I say, was their first Merchant they had to deal with, and these were the Goods he had to sell, (viz.) State Bills of Several Kinds, Annuities, Interests on Loans, Rents of the Town House, and the like; and here I must observe, that the performing this Wonder I am now to speak of, (viz.) of Restoring the publick

Credit, so as to bring a Sum so monstrously great as Fifteen Hundred Millions, and sunk so very low as from 60 to 65 per Cent. Discount, to be Saleable at a Par; nay to 10, 20, and 30 per Cent. advance, for that they would have been at, but Mr. Laws himself Checkt it; I say the Entertaining a thought that such a Scheme was practicable, and laying a Scheme to do it, was as great a Testimony of Mr. Laws's Genius and Capacity, as the Performance has been of his good Fortune.

It was a Sea, so full of dangerous Shoals, and Rocks, so subject to sudden Storms and Hurricanes, in a Word, so threatning of certain Shipwreck; that no Pilot but this alone, would ever have ventured to have Launched out in it.

But we must cease the

Wondering, and go back beyond Wonder it self, Mr. Laws had begun well, the Bank was Establish'd, and began to gain upon the World; the Credit of it, as I have already obferv'd, appear'd openly, and seem'd to be Invulnerable; it was founded upon a Substantial basis, nay, indeed the only basis that could support Publick Credit, (viz.) it always had the Money in Specie and in its own keeping, sufficient to answer all Demands; upon this almost any thing might be undertaken.

But here I must not only give another instance of the masterly Genius of Mr. Laws, the Contriver of all these things, but must let the World see, that as no Design however good in it self, and adapted for the general good of our Country, can be without Enemies, Envy constantly opposing itself to the best Designs; so it was here; this Bank had a Formidable attack made upon it by a set of Merchants in Paris; some said they were Jews of Amsterdam, others that they were Dutch Merchants Dwelling in Paris, and others, that they were French; be that as it will, possibly they might be some of all the three sorts, for it could not be done by a few: The Sum they appeared with, being no less than Twenty five Millions. The Plot in a few Words was to muster up a large Number of Bills, to be Demanded altogether, and if possible to give a Blow to the Credit; in a Word, and to Express it in our Terms; to make a Run upon the Bank. The Particulars of the Story are related thus.

*'It was a little after the first advance of the Credit of the Royal Bank at Paris, of which Mr. Laws was the principal Director, as he really was the Father and Author of it; some Merchants in Paris (it was reported to be a Plot Originally laid at Amsterdam, or more properly in Holland) whether it was so or not we do not affirm, but this is certain, that they were chiefly Dutch Merchants who appeared in it at Paris; we say, some Merchants at Paris having some time before Concerted their Measures to give a blow to the Bank, Treasured up a number of Bank Bills, to the Sum of Twenty five Millions as some say, others Twenty two Millions of Livres, and appear*

*altogether, tho' in several forms, as of separate Persons and Interest, at the Bank, just at the same Hour, to Demand the Money, for those Bills.*

*The Clarks at the Bank Surpriz'd with the appearance of so many Eminent Merchants, and with such great Demands, answer'd, that they should be paid, but desir'd them to wait a little till they could send to Mr. Laws the Director, that they might have his orders how to proceed in paying them; accordingly they immediately acquainted Mr. Laws with the thing, he paus'd a while at the thing, and without any Supprize, after a little Consideration, bid them go back and tell the Merchants they should all be paid, and bid the Clarks begin the payment, and to pay them all in Lowes d'or's or Pistoles, and that he would come Immediately to the Office, which he did, having first been to tell the Regent his Scheme, and had the assistance of the Royal Treasury, and of the General Farmers, for about One hundred fifty thousand Pistoles, in Specie, if he had wanted them; which however he did not.*

*Accordingly the Clarks begun the payment, and it held till the next day afternoon; by which time, as we have the Story, an Edict was procured and actually made Publick to reduce the Lowis d'or's from 16 to 15 Livres, which loss fell instantly upon the Merchants, while they had, above a Million and a quarter of Pistoles in their Hands in Specie, and the Bank having stood its Ground, had most of those Pistoles in their Cash again in a few Days.'*

This was a home Thrust at the Bank, but as it was Parry'd with so much Art, and the Loss of it turn'd upon the Contrivers, it Establish'd the very Foundation which it was form'd to shake, and gave such a Credit, not only to the Bank, but to Mr. Laws the principal Manager and Director in that Exigence, that it secured them both from any future attempts of that nature; it also let the World see, that not only they were strong in the substance of their Cash, and able to answer all Demands, and not only that they had a superior Genius at the head of their management, which was always able to Counter act their Projects, but that they had the Government hard and fast to support them upon all Occasions; and this indeed was such a Foundation, that when the Mississipi or West-India Company was first formed, it was apparent, that tho' there was little or nothing in the thing itself yet there were other Engraftments to be made upon it by the Government, that it could not miss of Success; and that in a Word, that Mississipi was only the Name, but that the Thing was intended to be a Fund of Credit, upon which the sinking Fortunes of the Government were to rise again.

The first thing we found gave life to the Company was the Coinage, the next was the

Farm of Tobacco, either of these were Things of a magnitude sufficient to have given Credit to any new Fund; but seem'd to be but Trifles in the hand of the Company, who apparently aimed at the General Management of the Revenues of France: However, as the undertaking of the Coinage was a vast thing in its Nature, so the manner of the Contract, the Prudence with which the Company engag'd in it, the visible Advantage which the Company would make by it, and above all, the Advance which they were to make to the King for it, were such Great things that it startled the World, and they began to talk of the West-India Company, as of an Opulent Powerful Body, that being Headed by an Enterprising Man, who apparently had undertaken what never Man before him undertook, and perfectly understood what he had undertaken, had more in it than was at First imagin'd, and would arrive to some greater hight than had been thought possible.

Upon these Thoughts, and the Reputation of the Company's undertaking beginning to be Popular, everybody enquired into it, and the farther they look'd into it, the better they began to like it; and this set People first upon buying the Stock, and the Number of the Buyers, by the meer nature of the thing, would rise the Value.

Now it appear'd every day more and more, that Mr. Laws had lay'd his measures right when he gave away his Pistoles, as I have said above, to have the refusal of the Stock at 100 per Cent. for on a sudden the Stock jumpt up to Par, and in three or four days more to 150. Had Mr. Laws stay'd the full time, and not Demanded the Stock till it was Advanc'd as we now see it risen, he must in all probability have lost the Advantage he had due to him, seeing very few of the Persons he had Contracted with would have been able to make good a difference of a Stock risen from under a Hundred to a Thousand: But as he shew'd his Moderation in Demanding the Stock, within the advance of about 200 per Cent. the Persons who lost that Money to him, were soon made amends if they had any Stock, by finding it still rising upon their hands to a prodigious degree in a few days.

We must take the liberty to make a Digression here, to the Volatile Temper of the French Nation, whose levity only can account for what we are now to take notice of, and the warmth of the French Temper must indeed be answerable for the running up an Imaginary Stock; for except about 37 or 40 Livres, upon a 100 in the first Subscription, it was no other to such a sudden and such an unaccountable extravagant hight.

This warmth of the French Temper, which prompts them to push things up to the Extremity, was certainly the Reason, I mean the Original Reason of the sudden Advance of these things, for as yet there was no weight in the things themselves, that could bear any proportion to the New Credit they assum'd: The Company had indeed engag'd with the Government, and had taken the Coinage of the King, as above, and in Nine years it was calculated they would get near Fifty Millions by their Contract, provided also the Government kept their Word with them, and made no new alterations in the Coin to their Detriment: But even this, in an Arbitrary Administration, such as that of France is known to be, was not so certain, but that the Risque of it was worth something to Ensure; and all the Doubt that could be justly rais'd on that Head, pleaded in abatement to the Credit of the Company.

It must therefore, I say, be placed to the account of the fluttering, rash Disposition of the People of France, that a thing who had yet no farther or greater prospect than that of the Coinage, should in a few days mount up its Credit to near 200 per Cent, upon the Value.

But as we are immediately to see things more prodigious than this, let us Discharge our selves of this Particular first, that we may clear things as they go; The Arret for Granting to the Company the Coinage, as above, will fully describe the Circumstances of their Contract, and the View of Advantages they had by it; and therefore I cannot go on, till I have given it at large, as follows:

*July 16. 1719.*
*Extract of the Registers of the Council of State.*

*The King having by his Letters Patents of the Month of August, 1717, established a Trading Company under the Name of the West Company, and by his Edict in May last reunited to the said Company the Trade of the East-India, China, &c. his Majesty sees with Satisfaction, that that Company takes the best Measures for securing the Success of its Establishment; that they send a great Number of Inhabitants to the Country of Louisiana, which was granted them; that many private Persons make Settlements in, that Colony, and send thither Husbandmen, Tillers, and other Handicraft-men, to manure and improve the Land, sow Corn, plant Tobacco, breed Silk-worms, and do whatever is necessary to improve that Country. Furthermore, his Majesty being informed that the India Company is at great Charges for transporting the said Inhabitants, and furnishing the Colony with Meal and other Necessaries till the Land afford a sufficient Quantity of Provision for their Subsistance: That the said Company sends thither all sorts of Goods and Merchandize to render the Life of the Inhabitants more comfortable, and that for preventing Abuses too frequent in Colonies, they have taken Care to settle the Price thereof at a moderate Rate by a general Tariff, which they have sent thither to be affixed in their Store-houses and Magazines; that they have ordered the Biasters or Pieces of Eight to be receiv'd by their Officers on the foot of five Livres, and the other Silver Bullion in Proportion, which Dispositions have appeared so wise and necessary, that his Majesty has resolved to favour the Execution thereof, and knowing that the exchanging of Goods not being sufficient to carry on Commerce to its full Extent, and that it is necessary in the beginning of Establishments of this Nature, to give them all possible Protection and Countenance, his Majesty has resolv'd to supply the said Company with a Sum of Bank Bills, to enable the Inhabitants of Louisiana to Trade amongst themselves, and bring into France the Fruits of their Labour, Oeconomy and Industry, without any Risque or*

*Charge: And his Majesty being willing to indemnify the said Company, for the Price of the Pieces of Eight in the Louisiana, and for the Expences they are at for the Establishment and Support of that Colony, he has thought fit to order all the Pieces of Eight and other Bullion that shall be imported by the said Company from the Louisiana, to be received at his Mints at their full Value. Therefore his Majesty being in the Council, with the Advice of Monsieur the Duke of Orleans, Regent, has ordered, and Orders, &c.*

*The Articles of this Arrest are to the following effect: 1. That the, Treasurer of the Bank shall deliver to the India Company the Sum of Twenty five Millions of Livres in Bank Bills, taking a Receipt of the Cashier of the said Company, to be sent to the Louisiana. 2. That in order that the said Bills be distinguished from others, the Numbers shall be kept by the Treasurer of the Bank, and the said Bills shall be sealed with the Seal of the India Company, instead of the Seal of the Bank. 3. That the said Bills being returned to France, shall be paid as well as other Bank Bills, by the Receivers of the King's Revenues, and afterwards acquitted by the Cashier of the Company, and by him brought to the Treasurer of the Bank, who shall deliver them new Bank Bills to be sent to the Louisiana, to the Value of the others. 4. The Owners of the said Bills must take the precaution to indorse them, that they may not be paid to any other but such who are to receive the Payment thereof; but in case they are lost by Shipwreck, or stoln, &c. the owner upon making a Declaration thereof to the Cashier of the Company, who is to enter the Number of the Bills lost, or supposed to be lost, shall receive the Value, thereof at the Expiration of five Years, according to the Declaration of the 4th of December, 1718. 5. And in order to indemnify the said Company for the Charges they are at for settling the Plantations in Louisiana, and for the Prices they give for the Pieces, of Eight, his Majesty orders that the said Pieces of Eight brought from those Plantations be receiv'd at his Mint at the rate of Sixty Livres per Mark, and in case of Alteration in the Price of the Coyn of the Kingdom, the Value of the said Pieces of Eight shall be paid Weight for Weight in the Species that shall be coyned or reformed, without any Diminution for the Charges thereof; and thereof as to the other Bullion, the same shall be receiv'd and paid at the Mint at the same Price as the Pieces of Eight, upon producing a Certificate from the General Directors of the said Company, that the said Pieces of Eight and other Bullion were shipped off in the Country of Louisiana, and belong to the said Company. Done in the Council of State, July 16. 1719.*

*Signed Fleuriau.*

## *July 25. 1719. Abstract of the Registers of the Council of State.*

*The King having ordered in Council his Edict in May, 1718. whereby new Species of Gold and Silver are ordered to be made, to be laid before him, and his Majesty being informed, that besides the good effects the Coyning thereof has produc'd, other considerable Advantages may be expected from the particular Attention to be given to its Continuation. Among the several Proposals that have been made to him on this Matter, none has appeared more Advantagious than the Proposition of the Directors of the India Company, who offer to pay to his Majesty Fifty Millions of*

*Livres in Specie, in fifteen equal successive payments from Month to Month, the first beginning on the first of October next, and the last the 1st of December, 1720. Upon Condition that the said Company shall enjoy for Nine years together to begin from the first of August next, the Benefit and Advantage arising from the old Species and Bullion that shall be brought to the King's Mints to be coyn'd into new Species. His Majesty is so much the more inclined to accept the Proposals of the said Company, because they may better and more and conveniently than private Men import Species and Bullion out of Foreign Countries, and that consequently they may get a greater Advantage thereby than his Majesty could get if the*

*Coinage of the new Species was continued upon his own Account; and furthermore considering that the Profit that will arise out of the same will be divided between great numbers of his Majesty's Subjects, concerned in the said Company, and that a Supply of certain and ready will enable his Majesty to pay the Arrears of Pensions and other Expences, His Majesty, with the Advice of Monsieur the Duke of Orleans, Regent, has ordained, and ordains as follows:*

*This Arrest contains four Articles, which are to this effect: 1. His Majesty accepts the offer made by the India Company of the Sum of Fifty Millions of Livres, to be paid in Fifteen successive Months, to begin from the first of October next, at the, rate of 3,333,333 Livres, 6 Pence, 8 Deniers per Month, and orders that, the same be brought to his Royal Treasury, and that the Receipt given by the Keeper thereof be a sufficient Discharge to the said Company, without being accountable to the Chamber of Accounts. 2. Besides the said Sum of Fifty Millions, the Company is to be at all the charges of the Coinage, Remittance, &c. such as the King does actually pay. 3. Upon these Conditions, the King grants to the said Company all the Profits and Advantages that shall accrue from the Coining into new Species of Gold and Silver in his Mints, the old Species of France, the Species of Foreign Countries, and Bullion that shall be imported, what Sum soever they may amount to, on the foot and manner regulated by the Edict of May, 1718, for Nine Years together, to begin from the first of August next. 4. His Majesty declares, that during the said Nine Years, he will not make any Augmentation in the Price of the Species, nor lessen the Standard of his Coin upon any Pretence whatsoever, and that in cafe of any Diminution, he will lower the Bullion and old Species proportionably. Done in, the Council of State, July 25. 1719.*

It was some Weeks that the Credit of the Company fed upon this Undertaking; and Mr. Laws, who prudently gave every thing time to Work, let it run on some time, upon this view only till the People began to talk a little dubious about it; That it was true, the Company would get Money by the Coinage, but it must be in a length of time; and that this was not so considerable that the Stock should mount up to such a hight upon that Advantage only.

When these things began to be the subject of Discourse, Mr. Laws began to think of playing another Mine; for I am to suppose all along this Gentleman to have built his whole fabrick in his Imagination at once, and to have Digested every part even from the beginning in his Thoughts, but resolved to bring every thing about by just degrees, and to give every thing that he started into the World its full scope, to extend it self to the utmost.

On a sudden then, for all his

Motions were like Mines, sprung from beneath, not the least Notice being given of any thing till it burst out like a sudden Fire; I say, on a sudden he Declares at his Levee, which now began to be as Great as that of a Publick Minister, that the King had United the East-India Company to that of Mississippi or the West-India and immediately after, that is to say, the next morning an Arret of the King's Council appear'd by which the two Companies were United and the Stock of the East-India Company Ingrafted into the other Company, as by the Arret itself is best explain'd, and which has in it several Clauses infinitely to the Advantage of the Company, in Trade as well as in Credit, tho' even in this Conjunction, and all the Advantages of a Commerce to the East-Indies encreased as they might be able to encrease it; were in themselves but remote things, and could produce no great things for some Years to come, and therefore could not be an addition of an Intrinsick worth, on which to raise such an immense inexpressible fund of Credit as immediately appear'd: But let us go on gradually, and first look into the Arret itself, that we may the better judge of what it is the Company enjoy, and what they ought to be valued at upon that particular Account. The Arret is as follows:

*Extract of the Registers of the Council of State.*

*Upon the Representation made to the King in Council by Directors of the India Company in Name of the said Company; That if the King was pleased to vacate and make void the Lease or Contract of the General Farms made in favour of Aymart Lambert for six Years, which begun on the first of October 1718. and of which the first Year will expire on the first of October next, and to substitute the said Company in the room of the said Lambert, under the Name of such Person as they shall think fit, under the Security of the Company for the remaining five Years of the Lease aforesaid: And to grant to the said Company four other Years, which will make a Lease of Nine Years, to begin from the first of October next, and end on the first of October 1728, with Power to the said Company to continue or vacate the Leases made by the said Lambert, as they shall think fit, the said Company will give over and above what was given by the said Lambert, three Millions five hundred thousand Livres for every Year during the said Term of Nine Years, insomuch that instead of Forty eight Millions five hundred thousand Livres, the said Lambert paid every Year for the said General Farms, the said Company will pay Yearly Fifty two Millions, and besides will perform all the Clauses and Conditions contain'd in the Lease granted to the said Lambert: That the better to shew to his Majesty the desire of the said India Company, to contribute by their Credit to the Ease of the*

*State, they offer to lend to the King Twelve hundred Millions of Livres at the Yearly Interest of three per Cent. to be employed towards the reimbursing and redeeming the perpetual Rents or Annuities, and other Debts assigned on the Aids and Gabells, the Tailles, the General Receipts of the Revenues, the Comptrolling or Registring of Acts passed by Notaries and Exploits, and on the Revenues of the Post-Office, together with the Reimbursements of the Rents or Shares on the Farms, the State-Bills, Bills of the Common Cash, and the Sums advanced for the Offices already suppressed or to be suppressed, which are not, or shall not be assigned upon any one Fund in particular: That in order to enable the said*

*Company to advance the said Twelve hundred Millions of Livres, his Majesty is desired to authorize and impower the said Company to borrow Twelve hundred Millions of Livres, for which they will deliver out Shares of Rents to the Bearer, to be paid by, the said Company, or Contracts of Annuities or Rents at the yearly Interest of three per Cent. which shall be advanced to them, and paid by the Cashier of the Company, to begin from the first of January next, following the Order of the Numbers of the Shares and the Date of the Contracts. That after the Company had furnished the Twelve Hundred Millions aforesaid, Commissioners appointed by his Majesty for that purpose, shall make and deliver to the said Company, one or more Contracts of perpetual Rent at three per Cent. per Annum, for the Sum of Twelve Hundred Million of Livres aforesaid, which Rents shall be assigned on the General Farms, to begin from the first of January, 1720. That therefore the said Company shall reserve, and keep in their own Hands the Annual Sum of Thirty Six Millions of Livres for the Payment of the said Rents or Annuities, during the Term of the Nine Years of their Lease, and after the Expiration thereof the Farmers of the General Farms, shall be oblig'd, in case the Company does not renew and Continue their Lease, to pay to the said India Company, the said Thirty Six Millions of Livres every*

*Year by Monthly Payments, at the Rate of Three Millions per Month: And lastly his Majesty is desired to be pleased to grant the Continuation for Fifty Years of all the Privileges that have been granted to the said Company, and of those granted to the several Companies that have been reunited to it. Whereupon the King in his Council, with the Advice of Monsieur the Duke of Orleans, Regent, has accepted and accepts the Offers of the India Company to his Majesty &c. and in Consideration thereof has ordained and ordains, &c. The Arrest contains seven Articles, whereby all the Demands of the Company are granted, and their Privileges are continued for Fifty Years, which are to end on the first of January*

*1770, upon Condition that the Company shall fully pay all the Debts of the old Company, both in France and the Indies, &c.*

It is not to be express'd with what surprise, and even astonishment the World look'd on at these steps of Mr. Laws, his Fame for an Enterprizing Man was now Establish'd, and those who had before run pretty much upon his Credit, and talk'd to his prejudice among the common People began to say now he was *Une habile homme*, and that he was capable of great things; for the noise of this new East-India Company spread like a Clap of Thunder far and wide, and People began to see a new world of Profit attending it, the East-India Trade being carried on in Great-Britain and in Holland to such a magnitude and to so much advantage as we an know it to be done.

All this while the on looking World regarded in their Calculations nothing but the ProfitsofTrade,andtheAdvantages the Company might make by great Returns, having a Capital Stock, and a good Oeconomy in their Affairs, keeping their eyes upon the Number of Ships to be sent annually to the East-Indies, the Extent of their Colonies and Plantations in the Louisiana and on the Banks of the Mississippi, what Rents in time shall accrue to the Stock, and what Annual Incoms the Company would receive, whereby they would be enabled to make Dividends proportion'd to 250 per Cent. upon their Subscriptions as they were then advanc'd, not imagining what was yet behind.

But Mr. Laws, whose Views lay another way, regarded all these things, only as they tended to raise a Fund of Credit at home, which was from the beginning the Point he aim'd at, leaving all other things to work their own way; not but the remotest Prospects concurr'd to answer the same End, and a Complication of Advantages however remote, serv'd to bring about the great Point, viz. The making the Credit of the whole to rise beyond imagination, and sufficient to answer all the great Things he had still in View.

The Stock was now risen to an excessive hight, from 325 to 350 per Cent. and now was the Time for Mr. Laws to let the world see what a Fund of Credit is able to do, and to make good the undoubted Maxim, That a Fund of Credit, is a Fund of Money, and able to make it self equal to all the Money in the World; for now was the time to strike the blow, that Coup d'Eclat, which should surprize and astonish the World, and which will forever be spoken of as an Action, that the World never heard of the like before.

Nor did Mr. Laws bring it out all at once, but suffer'd it to be discours'd of gradually, That the Company was about to take upon them the management of the King's Revenue; in a few days after, for Mr. Laws never suffer'd the Town to be Master of his Measures before they were ripe, but it had not been long spoken of that the Company would take upon them the management of the Revenue, when at once, just as before, an Arrest was published, Dissolving the Leases of the General Farmers of the Revennue, tho' their Leases had five Years to run, and vesting the whole Collection in the new East-India Company.

As an Inducement to this, the Company undertake to encrease the payment to the King, no less than four Millions a Year, a Sum too Considerable not to be Vallued: But at the end of this comes a Clause, which none but such a Man as Mr. Laws could have ventur'd upon, a thing Posterity will look back upon as a Romance, and which no History can give any thing like it, namely, the paying the King's Debts, that is to say, the Company to take upon them at once the Discharging all all the King's Debts upon whatsoever

Doubtful Funds, upon whatever precarious Circumstances they stood, whatever Discounts they were at, all are to be transferr'd at once from the Royal Treasury, where they would never have been able to Discharge them, to the Treasury of the Company where they are to be paid at Demand.

Two things make this Undertaking a prodigy of management, the like of which was never heard of before:

1. The King's Debts amounted to about Fifteen Hundred Millions.

2. The Company had not any Fund of Money, or the Value of Money to pay them with.

But before I go on, I must go back to the Arrests or Proclamations,

Directing the Execution of this unparallel'd Contract, which by mistake is already placed Page [65]. but should have come in here.

Here is such a blow struck, as the World never heard of before; and in this very stroke we may behold the Power of Credit, and what immense Structures may be built, and Mr. Laws has built upon this single foundation, by which he has restor'd a Government overwhelm'd with Debt and which was turn'd Bankrupt to the People, and has deliver'd a Nation oppress'd with Taxes, in such a manner, and in so short a time, that Posterity will never believe the relation; but will all look like a Fable or Romance in their Eyes.

The Arret or Act of the King's Council above mention'd, for

the settling this Point, tells us expresly what the Company are to do, and expresses the Sum which they are to lend the King for the doing it, (viz.) That they should lend the King Twelve Hundred Millions of Livres at 3 per Cent. and afterwards they added three Millions more, for the paying off all the publick Debts, and strictly ties them down to so punctual a Discharge of those Debts, and of all the Sallaries of the Officers, &c. that it shall be wholly in the choice of the Persons who are to be paid, whether they will accept of the Company's Bonds, or have their Ready Money paid them. But the Arrets do not at all meddle with the Method by which the Company shall raise such an Infinite mass of Money to pay, but supposes the Money shall all be actually ready in Cash, in Specie to pay, only gives the Company Power to Borrow such a Sum, that is to say, if any one will lend it; for they do not oblige anyone to Lend, much less to accept the Company's Security for the Debt; for that would but have been exchanging the Government for the Company, and leaving the Debt still in being.

Nor on the other hand was here the least Consideration to the Company for so great an Advantage to the Government, as that of clearing them at once of all the publick Debts; had the Company reserv'd but the small advantage of One per Cent. on the Interest as they were empowered to Borrow, the 1200 Millions at 3 per Cent. had the Government paid 4 per Cent. which had been just 1 per Cent. Gain, there had been then some visible Profit, (viz.) there had been Twelve Millions per Annum in the Company's Pocket, to have enabled them, or help'd at least, to make some proportion'd Dividends to the monstrous advance of their Stock.

But the whole Scene may be one continued Prodigy, they seek no Advantage, they Demand no more than Three per Cent. and propose to Borrow, if they want it, at Three per Cent. acting in every part of it upon the foundation of Publick Service, without Gain to themselves.

But neither is this all, for we shall presently see them not only take no Surplus of Interest, no Gain of Interest more than they pay; But we shall see the Credit rising to an immense hight, and the

Company growing Powerful by the Assistance of the Government, and the management of Mr. Laws their Director: I say, we shall see the following Mysteries, or, indeed, Miracles, wrought in the compass of a few Weeks, Things as incredible as the greatest Impossibility in Nature could be thought to be; things which now they are done, they are as a Dream even to those that see them; even the People who have the Money in their hands, and who has receiv'd their antient Debts, so long given over, so effectually despair'd of, they look amaz'd, and Consider again and again, whether they are awake or asleep, they handle it, weigh it, and roll it about, as if they would try whether it is really Gold or Air; whether there is no Magic, no Necromancy in it or not; and I am told of one to whom the Government ow'd Ten Thousand Crowns, which he would have been glad to have sold for Two Thousand five Hundred, being an Arrear for Secret Service only, that caused an Iron Chest to be bought, and put the Money into it, then drove Posts into the Ground in his Cellar, and chain'd the Iron Chest down to the Stakes, then chain'd it also to the Wall, and Barricadoed the Doors and Window of the Cellar with Iron, and all for fear, not of Thieves to Steal the Money, but for fear the Money, Chest and all should flyaway into the Air; For he said he could never believe it was Money. But to return to the Particulars, which I say have been done by this Company, subsequent to this new Arret of paying the publick

Debts: We have seen them since that do strange things indeed!

1. We have seen them bring the People to refuse payment, or decline payment of what they would before have given half the Debt to be secur'd of.

2. The State Bills that were before little better than wast Paper, made worth 10 per Cent. and 20 per Cent. above Par.

3. We have seen them Gain Thirteen Hundred and Fifty Millions of Money in less than a Months time by selling the Air, and putting a real Value upon an imaginary value.

4. We have seen the King's Revenue augmented to Millions a year, by abating the Taxes to the People.

5. We have seen the General

Farms rais'd Four Millions a Year to the King, and yet twelve Millions a Year paid less by the People.

6. We have seen them Pay Fifteen Hundred Millions of Debt for the King, without one Penny of Money.

7. Lastly, We have seen a private Gentleman raise himself by the Dexterity of this Management, to be the greatest Subject in the World; to have all the Nobility, the Princes, the Publick Ministers, and even the Government it self at his beck, and above 300 Coaches in a Morning at his Levee, himself behaving with all the Modesty and Humility imaginable; not Elevated by his good Fortune, not Hurried or Discompos'd by the application to so much business, but Calm and

Cool, always present to himself, answering briefly and pertinently to every new Discourse, receiving Six or Seven Hundred Gentlemen in a Morning, dispatching every Business with a Readiness inimimitable, perfectly Compos'd and Retir'd, and every Day producing new Wonders in the great Affair of the Publick which is upon his Hands.

I return to the Stock, and the proceeding of the Company: As the Advantages of Publick business thus flow'd in, the Credit of the Stock necessarily Advanc'd; and we were surpriz'd in England to find that every Post the Price started up whole Hundreds in a Day, till at length we saw the Stock up at 1150 per Cent. 1200, and since that to 2050 per Cent.

Now was the Juncture of Mr. Laws to give the blow he had in View, the multitude of People who came every Hour to Paris, and run their Money into the Stock, made his Project not Rational only but Natural, (viz.) That they might enlarge the Capital Stock by Engrafting a farther Subscription, and that the New Subscribers might have Encouragement to Subscribe, they should be allowed to Subscribe at 1000 Livres each, Original Stock.

Pursuant to this Resolution, an Arrest was published, empowering the Company to take new Subscriptions upon the first Foot of the Stock for 50 Millions, the Subscribers paying 10000 Livres each; and that I may explain it as I go, you are to understand, that for the Ten Thousand Livres, the Subscribers has Credit in the Companies Books for one Action or Share, that is to say, for One Hundred Livres Original Stock.

This being the Case, it is easie to Calculate what the Company's Gain by this new Subscription, but of that in its Place: In the mean, time it is to observ'd, that so eager were the People to throng in their Money into the Stock, that they were ready to tread one another to death to get to the Books, and it was the greatest Favour in the world to be admitted; so that the Books were not only fill'd up in about Six Hours, but if there had been room for Two Hundred Millions, it would have been fill'd up at the same time.

No sooner was the Subscription declared full, and no more hands to be taken, but those who could not get in their Money, falls to work with those that had, and buy of them part of what they had subscrib'd, and this rais'd the Price so, that the new Stock rise immediately 100 per Cent. even the same day that it was subscrib'd.

As this had been clos'd with so eagerly, and with so much ardour by the People, Mr. Laws, who knew very well how to make his Advantage of the Temper of the People, obtains a second Order for 50 Millions more, and in a Word had it fill'd with the same eagerness and forwardness as before, and after this a third of 50 Millions; the Arrest of these Subscriptions are publick in our Papers, and will shew something of the Proof of what I have affirm'd, of the forwardness of Subscribers;

they are indeed too long to be Copied here, neither is it of great use to us to see the Form, which is only what is usual in the Publick Acts on like Occasions.

It is now proper to Examine what Immense Gain accrues to the Company by these Subscriptions, as also the Original Stock as then Advanc'd: I begin with the Subscriptions, which, as above were taken in at a 1000 Livres upon each 100 Livres Original Stock.

If then the Subscription was for Fifty Millions Stock, at 100 Livres each Subscription, this advanc'd to a 1000 Livres, each Stock amounts to no less than 500 Millions of Livres; so that the Company receiving 1000 Millions of Livres, for 50 Millions Original Stock, advance, and are clear Gainers by the Subscription no less than 450 Millions of Livres, and this doubled by the second Subscription of 50 Millions make the Company's Gain amount to 900 Millions of Livres, and that to a third, it makes it 1350 Millions.

Add to this, the first Stock of the Company was much of it Subfcrib'd by the Government itself, by the King, by Mr. Laws as in the Company's Name, and being sold since at 1000 and 1100 per Cent. has put, as I am credibly inform'd, above 200 Millions into their Pockets; besides what Mr. Laws is said to have Gain'd for his private Account.

It will now be no longer a Wonder how, and with what Coin the Company should undertake to pay off 1500 Millions of Debt, or how they could begin to pay, as was the Case, Four Months before the appointed Time, for here is 1340 Millions Clearly gain'd, *Tout d'une Coup*, at one blow, to go on upon the payment with whenever they pleas'd, besides what was to come; and no body then doubted but that Mr. Laws would set up a third Subscription; but he found it convenient to stop here for the present, and not only not to take a farther Subscription, but to put that out of doubt, he obtain'd a publick Arret declaring, that there should be no new Subscriptions granted.

But in this new Experiment Mr. Laws found himself a little embarrass'd for there being such a run for their New Subscriptions, there were Consequently no Buyers, or fewer Buyers than before for the Old Stock, everyone having, as we say in England, a Penny for a new Shop; neither was this all, but as the new Subscribers paid but 100 Livres down upon their Subscription, the rest being allow'd to be paid in by Equal payments in Nine Months, 100 Livres per. Month, it was with much ease subscrib'd, because they paid, as above, but 100 Livres for an Action, whereas whoever bought an Old one, was oblig'd to pay 1000 Livres down, this carried away the Buyers from the Old Stock, but this likewise was not all, for those who had a mind to subscribe to the New Stock, on purpose to Sell out again, and Jobb them about, sold out the Old Stock, because for two Old Actions, for which, when sold the Seller receiv'd 2000 Livres, he might with that Money

Subscribe, or buy Subscriptions for 20 Shares or Actions in the New; and laying down the first payment, get to Quinquampoix Street, the Exchange-Alley of Paris, and selling them again at 1100 Livres each, put 2000 Livres in his Pocket, and be just where he was.

These Things had their Influence upon the Old Stock, and there being abundance wanted to Sell, and few to Buy, the Price fell at once, and indeed began to fall so Considerably, that from 1250 it fell to 760, which was a threatning Article; but Mr. Laws gave a new Life to it all at once, for he perceiving it, and knowing it would run too fast for him to stop it if it was not taken in time, applied an immediate Remedy to it which could not fail to answer his end, this was to publish, and fix it up at the Door of the Bank, and at other publick places of the City, That the Company would take in all the Old Shares that any Man was willing to part with, at 900 Livres per Share.

This was another Testimony of the Masterly Genius of Mr. Laws; for as soon as ever this publication was made the Old Stock mounted again, and Sold Currently for 1050 and 1030 or thereabout, no body coming, or but few to sell them.

Thus he warded off the blow: But this was one Reason why he durst not venture to form any additional Subscriptions, and a good Reason too: But from this time forward, the Stock is Grown up to a Prodigy of 2050 per Cent. It is true it has sunk a little on the approach of the time of Payment for the first Three Months, which is to be paid in the first of January, viz. 300 Livres per Share, and this for want of Money has sunk the Stock to about 1850; but Mr. Law, that never wants a Remedy for these Diseases, immediately calls a meeting of the Directors, and agrees to declare a Dividend of Profits to amount to 6 per Cent. upon the Stock, which tho' it be a Triffle on the present advanc'd Price, yet was really Considerable in it self, and amounts to a very great Sum, no less than Six Millions and upwards: However 'tis agreed that the Company have really gained near 100 Millions Extraordinary, by selling her own Subscriptions, and buying and selling her own Stock; so that they may very easily Divide 20 per Cent. on the 1st Stock, which would have been 1 per Cent. upon the present Advance; but of this hereafter. This is a brief Account of the prodigious Rise and Greatness of the East-India Stock, and of its present State and Condition.

It remains to give some account of its progress, and the steps Mr. Law is taking to establish the Trade which it has in View; for tho' indeed the Trading part has been the least of Mr. Law's design, yet as it is the Denominating quallity of the Company, and they are called the Mississippi and East-India Company, he pushes this part also.

The Proceeding of the Mississippi part, is partly seen in the Arret of the Council, misplaced by mistake, Pag. [50], and which ought to have been placed here: Wherein the Bank gives, or rather lends the Company 25 Millions in Bank-Bills, for small Sums to be Current in the Colony of Louisania or Mississippi, and partly in the multitude of People which are every Day all for Planting sent thither.

As for the East-India Trade, we find them launching out into a Prodigious Trade that way, and sending out about Twenty Ships with Soldiers and vast Cargoes, to make Settlements, and place Factories in the East-Indies, and all the Twenty Ships to come Home Loden with things proper for the Trade they are upon.

These are great things it must be confest, but as I have said, these are not the chief end in View; Mr. Law's aims are at Popularity, and keeping up the Imaginary part which is raised to such a degree, as the Profit of Ten East-India Trades could not support, and which never can be supported without something that can bring in a Profit equal to 3 or 4 per Cent. per Annum, upon the 2000 per Cent. which it stands advanc'd.

To bring this to pass, we find he does every thing, and the Government in his behalf does every thing that can recommend them to the People, and particularly acts of Generous Charity, Publick Spirited Muneficence, taking off the heavy Taxes upon the ordinary Necessaries of Life and Convenience, by which the Poor, who are more Sensible of those things, are touch'd, and engage to Bless both the Person and the Undertaking.

Innumerable Projects are in his Head for publick good, he has already caused all the Turnpikes and Tole-bars at the entrance into the Streets of Paris to be taken down; an innumerable number of Collectors and Officers, that teiz'd the Poor for Money upon every Trifle that enter the City of Paris, are dismissed, the People pay nothing for Coals or Wood, or Turff to burn, Hay or Oats, or Straw for Horses, Flesh or Fish, Herbs or Garden Stuff, and Fruits or Wine to Drink; all Things go free into Paris, so that the Families live a fifth part cheaper than they did before; the very Duty on Fish, which is now abolished, brought in to the King two Millions a Year; but now as the Rents of the Town House of Paris are Reimbursed, and they have no more Annuities to pay, they have likewise no Taxes to Levy, and all is made free.

Besides these things; which are the Consequence of paying the publick Debts, he has new Projects of so many kinds, that it would require a large Book to give an account of them.

He has undertaken a New Canal, from the River Loyer to the Seine, to bring more Water into the latter, by the River Loyng, and answerable to the Canal de Briare, so to bring Vessels of large Burthens down those Rivers, and bring Wine and Brandy, and all bulky Goods quite from Nants in Bretaign, and from the Sea, as well as from the Inland Country about Orleans.

He has lay'd a Scheme to Reduce the River Seine to a

narrower Channel between Paris and Roan, that so the Channel may be deepen'd and kept clear, by which means Ships of good Burthen shall come up even to Paris it self, and Roan, Ships of 400 Tuns Burthen shall come freely up to the Town Key.

He has design'd to make Roan the Capital of all France, for Commerce, Navigation and Manufactures, all his East-India and Mississippi Trdae shall be carried on there, and the Magazines, Warehouses and Places for publick Sales, shall be fixt and built there; and as the City of Roan it self is not sufficient for the Number of People that will be drawn together by these Things, and by the Woollen Manufactures and Silk Manufactures, which he designs to settle there, he has projected, as Fame reports, a New City on the other Side of the Seine over against Roan, and a Stone Bridge of a most magnificent Structure, and which must be prodigious strong, the Water there being very deep and rapid.

This Tract would be far too short to give a full Scheme, even of this one design, a thing of such Magnitude as no Private Man ever undertook, or any Stock less than that of a Prince or of a Nation accomplished.

But all these things seem to me to be rather amusements to alarm the World, and make the Company Famous among Forreigners, than that they are to be really Executed.

And they have their end, for Foreigners are amused, and all the World seems to be running to Paris, the prodigious Sums Strangers layout in the Stock, and the Numbers that come to Negotiate there, has fill'd Paris with Money and with People, and Consequently with Trade; and they tell us there is nothing to be seen but New Coaches, New Equipages, New Liveries, and buying New Furniture; innumerable Families having been Enrich'd by this surprizing advance of Stock; in a word, they write from thence, that there are 1200 New Coaches set up in Paris, and half a Million of People come to the City more than was there before, so that no Lodgings are to be had; and they Build New Houses and Streets in every Place where they have Room.

When I begun this Work, it was not possible to imagine, but I might have given some account of the Ebb, as I have of the Flood of this Phantosme, for I can call it yet no more; its fate without question must come ere long, since there is no Foundation equal to the Structure that now stands upon it.

But the time is not yet, the little decrease, or fall which happened a few days ago, is not of the kind of that which must blow up the Machine; but it stop'd as above, by the appearance of an approaching Dividend of Profits: But this cannot support it long, it must fall at last, and all I can say of it at present can be only this, that when it comes *Great will be the fall of it*.

FINIS

ALSO AVAILABLE FROM NEWTON PAGE

ALSO AVAILABLE FROM NEWTON PAGE

**Letters to John Law**

A Letter to Mr. Law
The Case of Mr. Law Truly Stated
A Second Letter to Mr. Law

*Selected and introduced by*

Gavin John Adams

ISBN-13: 978-1-934619087

This collection of three uncompromising early eighteenth-century propagandist pamphlets documents the wildly contrasting reactions to Law's surprise return to Britain. Crafted by the most prominent journalists, commentators and political agitators of the day, each provides an invaluable contemporaneous social, political and historical record of the most remarkable story in financial history.

Newton Page books are available at all good bookstores and online book retailers. For more information about our books and how to order them, please visit our website:

NP
NEWTON PAGE

www.newtonpage.com

ALSO AVAILABLE FROM NEWTON PAGE

## The Financier Law

His Scheme and Times: A Graphic Description of the Origin, Maturity and Wreck of the Mississippi Scheme

André Cochut

ISBN-13: 978-1934619049

A richly contextual narrative of the life of John Law, a charismatic Scottish economist and murderer and who would escape execution and use his seemingly effortless financial genius to rise from obscurity to become the most powerful member of the French court, the controller of the French economy, and the richest man the modern world had ever seen.

ALSO AVAILABLE FROM NEWTON PAGE

## The Present State of the French Revenues and Trade

### And of the Controversy Betwixt the Parliament of Paris, and Mr. Law

John Law

ISBN-13: 978-1-934619131

First published in 1720, *The Present State of the French Revenues and Trade* was written to shine a favourable light upon John Law's Mississippi Scheme. It contains a series of letters written by Law which seek to defend the Mississippi Scheme, explain the principles upon which it was based, and attempt to assuage the damaging concerns and controversies which had been raised about its operation.

ALSO AVAILABLE FROM NEWTON PAGE

**The Mississippi Bubble**

A Memoir of John Law

Adolphe Thiers

ISBN-13: 978-1934619056

An established classic and authoritative historical analysis of the spectacular rise and fall of the most enigmatic genius in financial and economic history. It provides a compelling biographical narrative of John Law's life, a considered examination of his Mississippi Scheme, and enlightening accounts of both the Darien Expedition and South Sea Bubble.

ALSO AVAILABLE FROM NEWTON PAGE

**John Law of Lauriston**

Financier and Statesman, Founder of the Bank of France, Originator of the Mississippi Scheme

A. W. Wiston-Glynn

ISBN-13: 978-1934619032

The true story of a Scottish murderer, philanderer, gambler and abscondee who escaped his condemned cell in London to become the darling of the French economy, John Law of Lauriston is an account of the euphoria and wealth Law created by engineering the first stock market boom, and the despair, poverty and destruction which followed its inevitable crash.

ALSO AVAILABLE FROM NEWTON PAGE

**A Full and Impartial Account of the Company of Mississippi:**

Otherwise Call'd the French East India Company, Projected and Settled by Mr. Law

Anonymous

ISBN-13: 978-1-934619124

First published as a propagandist pamphlet (in both French and English) in 1720, it was not really an 'impartial account' at all, as it was commissioned, written and published primarily to both reassure existing investors, and encourage potential investors, of the advantages to be gained by becoming a shareholder in John Law's Mississippi Company .

Made in the USA
Las Vegas, NV
26 March 2026

44304614R00083